Moments
Remembered

Moments
Remembered

A 30-Day Devotional for Families

By Douglas Lim

Bladensburg, MD

Moments Remembered
Published by
Inscript Books
a division of Dove Christian Publishers
P.O. Box 611
Bladensburg, MD 20710-0611
www.dovechristianpublishers.com

Copyright © 2020 by Douglas Lim

Cover Design by Nadia Chatsworth

ISBN: 978-1-7348625-0-8

All rights reserved. No part of this publication may be used or reproduced without permission of the publisher, except for brief quotes for scholarly use, reviews or articles.

Scriptures quotations, unless otherwise marked, are from the Holy Bible, New International Version®, NIV® Copyright © 1973, 1978, 1984, 2011 by Biblica, Inc.® Used by permission. All rights reserved worldwide.

Scripture quotations marked NLT are taken from the Holy Bible, New Living Translation, copyright © 1996, 2004, 2015 by Tyndale House Foundation. Used by permission of Tyndale House Publishers, Inc., Carol Stream, Illinois 60188. All rights reserved.

Scripture quotation marked ESV is from the ESV® Bible (The Holy Bible, English Standard Version®), copyright © 2001 by Crossway, a publishing ministry of Good News Publishers. Used by permission. All rights reserved."

Published in the United States of America

To my loving wife and children, and
all families who put Christ at the center of their
lives

Acknowledgments

To my caring, loving, and supportive wife, Cindy, my deepest gratitude goes out to you. Your encouragement to move forward with this project was invaluable to me. God bless you always.

And to the publication team at Inscript Books, I would like to thank you again for the evaluation and acceptance of my work, and especially the effort put in at each step of the process.

Introduction

The devotionals in *Moments Remembered* speak about God's presence amid circumstances, often challenging ones, within the family circle. Each devotional uncovers a message and lesson from God for members of the family to reflect upon and apply to their lives.

These family devotionals can be read together for family sharing or read alone for personal reflection and prayer. The purpose of these devotionals is to help families rediscover God's love in their lives and to deepen their faith personally and as a family united together in Christ.

I hope that each member of the family will take time to read these devotionals and share how God has spoken to them and how He opened the eyes of our hearts to see more clearly His affection and daily care for each of us.

*But as for me and my household,
we will serve the Lord (Joshua 24:15).*

Day 1

Dark Rooms

> *The Lord is my light and my salvation—whom shall I fear? The Lord is the stronghold of my life—of whom shall I be afraid? (Psalms 27:1).*

The power went off in the house. Silence and darkness filled our home. I suddenly heard shouts from the children upstairs. The darkness frightened them, especially the monsters and ghosts the kids believed lurked in the dark. I lit candles and rushed upstairs. As the candle lights filled the room, they felt safe once again.

As adults, we also find ourselves in dark places. It is the darkness of everyday worries, of an unknown future, or a hurtful past that frightens us.

When Christ came into this world as the Light, He made it possible for us to see our way out of the darkness. But we must engage our faith and trust in Him for His light to illuminate the dark places and banish the fears. We do not know what the future holds, but our Master does. He is in control when we cannot be.

Like a child who wants his Mom and Dad to leave the lights on to feel safe, the Light of Christ will comfort all who seek Him.

Prayer

Heavenly Father, in moments of great distress, help me to open my heart wide to Your light that has the power to scatter the darkness of fear inside of me. Amen.

Day 2

Models of Faith

> *Fathers, do not exasperate your children; instead, bring them up in the training and instruction of the Lord (Ephesians 6:4).*

There is more I need to teach my children.

After dinner, my wife and I helped our kids with homework. We also set aside time to talk with them about school and their friends. We encouraged them to ask us questions about whatever was on their minds.

We often worried about their grades, health, and safety. But we should be concerned about something more. God commands us to teach our children about Jesus Christ and frequently reminds us how much it matters to educate them on the things of God.

As parents, our vocation is to lead our children to the Savior and ensure they arrive at the place of our heavenly Father. This means clearing a path for them to encounter Him. He called us to this mission as mothers and fathers from the beginning.

God wants us to be models of faith to our kids and cautions us not to block their path with our bad example. We need to walk with them on their faith journey until they are ready to walk with Jesus by themselves.

He equipped us to guide our children to love Christ through the guidance of the Holy Spirit and the power of grace. Joyful will be the day our Lord welcomes our children to walk alongside Him—and they follow.

Prayer

Lord, help me to become a better teacher of the faith to my children. Let my actions and words help them grow closer to You, our Savior. Amen.

Day 3

Second Chances

> *Just think how much more the blood of Christ will purify our consciences from sinful deeds so that we can worship the living God. For by the power of the eternal Spirit, Christ offered himself to God as a perfect sacrifice for our sins (Hebrews 9:14, NLT).*

I hated myself for using such cruel words. I told God how much I regretted causing my friend so much pain and embarrassment at school, and I asked for forgiveness. But I was not able to get over the guilt. I kept replaying the scene over and over in my mind, which made things worse.

Before long, I felt too ashamed—and stopped praying and going to church. Believing I didn't deserve forgiveness, I hid from God. Finally, it became clear I could never receive forgiveness nor start to feel better if I kept holding on to the guilt.

I began praying again. God showed me through Jesus' death on the cross that He forgave me—and I had a second chance to make things right.

Prayer

Lord, give me the courage to approach You when I have done something wrong. Help me to trust that if I pray to You with real regret, You will forgive me and guide me to do better next time. Amen.

Day 4

God's Promises

> *I am the way and the truth and the life. No one comes to the Father except through me (John 14:6).*

As I prepared for church Sunday morning, it occurred to me how often I play down the importance of God's presence in my life. He should be our inspiration to bring others to Christ, our fount for spiritual strength, and our reason for hope. God is everything. Through His Son, Jesus, the abundant life becomes possible for all who believe.

He is now at the right hand of God and wants us to make our home in the Kingdom of Heaven with Him someday. It is the reason He came down to us. It is the very reason He surrendered His life on the cross. Jesus Christ considers us His friends and promises to ask the Father to prepare a special place for us in His Heavenly Kingdom.

He also promised never to leave us alone. And on the day Jesus Christ rose to Heaven, He placed the Holy Spirit in the hearts of the faithful to always comfort and guide them. And when the time comes to make our way home, Christ will be there to accompany His followers to the front doorstep of the Father's house. We have a friend in Him. He will never forget a single one of His promises.

We are the Father's beloved sons and daughters through our faith in Jesus Christ. He waits for our safe return. It should give us hope and joy that the Father promised us a nice room upon our arrival.

The place searched for our whole lives will be unveiled in all its glory upon arrival. Death, sorrow, and pain come to a halt, our daily battles end, and peace and joy reign forever.

Prayer

Lord Jesus, let me never forget Your incredible promises. Help me to share with others the good news of these promises You have proclaimed to us. Amen.

Day 5

You're Priceless

> *Look at the birds of the air; they do not sow or reap or store away in barns, and yet your heavenly Father feeds them. Are you not much more valuable than they? (Matthew 6:26).*

As I rummaged up and down the aisles, the shoe department ahead with the caption "Prices Slashed" grabbed my attention. I tried on a pair of slip-on deck shoes. They fit and looked great—and a bargain at 25% off. But as I continued sampling other shoes, I noticed the value I placed on the slip-on vanished.

It became clear the shoes only had worth as long as nothing better came along. This principle applied to other items in my life, too, such as my navy-blue suit I wore quite often, the phone I glared at and swiped all day, and the car I practically lived in.

These possessions didn't have value in themselves but had value in comparison to other items of the same kind. On the other hand, there's one thing that does have absolute value—and it's each and every one of us.

But we weaken our self-worth when we compare our qualities to others. We may ask ourselves, "Since I'm not as educated, am I less admired?" "Since I'm not as successful, am I less valued?" "Since I'm not as popular, am I less respected?"

Jesus leaves us with no doubt we're valuable and carry within us a God-given dignity. Our value doesn't hinge on the qualities we may or may not have. We are beyond the comparison.

He didn't make a mistake when He created us. There is no need to compare ourselves to others to prove our worth.

Prayer

Lord, thank You for helping me understand how much I mean to You. Please remind me to never doubt or worry about not being valued enough in Your eyes. Amen.

Day 6

Soft and Comfy

> *Whoever finds their life will lose it, and whoever loses their life for my sake will find it (Matthew 10:39).*

I was an object at rest and wanted to remain that way.

Legs stretched out and feet propped up, I parked in front of the television on a warm summer evening, channel-flipping impulsively. Naturally, I purposefully placed a tall glass of iced tea and a bowl of nuts within easy reach.

But this particular evening was unlike previous nights. An uneasiness piqued my curiosity—a sensation strong enough to distract my stare away from the television screen.

I attributed the uneasiness to the tailwinds of the Holy Spirit's nudging again. It was suggestive of the winds that rushed through the upper room at Pentecost, penetrating the hearts of the disciples, after which they boldly proclaimed the gospel.

This prompting reminded me that my life had become too soft and comfy. I claimed to be a Christian, but I wondered if I'd honestly answered Christ's call to be a disciple. Something hindered me. I dreaded the cost.

I love my wife, children, gadgets, and channel-flicking. However, I loved my life and the many extras more than my Savior. The thought of losing the life I put together for myself and my family frightened me.

Being a true disciple demands some self-denial. For the devoted disciple, the way to union with Jesus calls for the cross—the cross that comes from following Him daily and faithfully. Only when we deny our life will we find the abundant life—a life with Christ.

God calls us to love Him more than others, including our family and friends. But this doesn't mean we must lessen the love we have for the people in our lives. On the contrary, the grace we've received from each act of self-denial for Him, whether big or small, makes it possible to live more fully for God and to love others even more.

Do something for God that makes you uncomfortable.

Prayer

Father in heaven, help us from getting so comfortable with the things of this world that we forget who we are as disciples in Christ. Remind us to keep You at the center of our lives. Amen.

My child, guard the commands of your father and do not forsake the instruction of your mother (Proverbs 6:20).

Day 7

The Principle of Least Effort

> *Rather, he must be hospitable, one who loves what is good, who is self-controlled, upright, holy and disciplined (Titus 1:8).*

As I stared at my phone, I started to consider how the advancement of technology has made our lives easier. We have online banking, online shopping, and online doctor's visits. Social media makes communication with friends so easy we no longer make time to see them in real life.

But reliance on technology has its drawbacks. It makes us seekers of ease and often supporters of a life apart from our Savior.

As Christians, our mission is to arrive at our heavenly Father's house, and this requires effort and dependence on God. He did not say we can get there any old way. And with little hope for a new gadget that can guide us from sin, we are left with our free will choices to follow Christ or not.

Fortunately, God provided us with something more powerful than any electronic device. It's called willpower. By saying "no" to temptation, we strengthen our willpower muscles and build up a reserve of spiritual power to fall back on when tempted.

God wants us to exercise willpower when tempted by our culture to worship power, prestige, and possessions, like electronic devices, instead of Him. When we turn toward His Son and the grace He provides, God will supercharge our willpower to resist temptation.

Our Shepherd does not want us lost in a life of ease and sin to the extent that we no longer welcome Him in our lives.

Prayer

Lord, help me to activate my willpower when tempted. Only by Your grace and love am I able to do what is right. I thank You for Your teachings, which helps me from getting lost in this world of electronic devices. Amen.

Day 8

Thrown in the Deep End

> *He measured off another thousand, but now it was a river that I could not cross, because the water had risen and was deep enough to swim in—a river that no one could cross (Ezekiel 47:5).*

It can be terrifying to try something we have never done before, whether it is our first bike ride without training wheels, our first drive on the highway with Mom, or our first speech in front of a room of strangers.

After I learned how to swim, it took me a while before I gathered up the courage to plunge into the deep end of the pool. I was sure I would flail around and then sink like a rock.

God's purpose often puts us into deep waters. He calls us to move from the safety of the kiddie end of the pool and head toward the deep end. If we choose to paddle only in waist-deep water, we miss the chance to witness His grace and power at work.

In the deep recesses of life is where we find His best work. It is God's way to prepare us for the next chapter in our walk with His Son. God does not put us in deep waters to see us go down but to deepen our faith and grow our trust.

Do we trust that God will not let us drown? Believing in His protection and care for each one of us, we can have the power to swim through the choppy waters of life. When we do, we'll emerge on the other side with a newfound strength—a new perspective and a new spiritual lesson on how to stay afloat when we find ourselves in the depths of life's struggles.

Prayer

Father, I often ignore Your nudges to try something new and unexpected. Please give me the courage to embrace the circumstances You place me in. Do not let fear prevent me from taking a step forward. Amen.

Day 9

Where I Found God

> *Be still, and know that I am God! I will be honored by every nation. I will be honored throughout the world (Psalms 46:10, NLT).*

After swimming in a relay race, my heart started pounding. When I woke up in the hospital, my parents told me I had passed out. The doctors said my competitive swimming days were over. My Junior Olympics dream shattered.

I spend many hours in a quiet hospital room. Quiet seemed strange to me, but somehow it allowed me to think about God. After leaving the hospital, I became angry a lot. I didn't understand why this had to happen and blamed God for ending my dream.

Later, during a check-up at the hospital, I recalled the quiet I experienced in my hospital room—the place where God seemed to be. When I got home, I went to my room, turned off my phone, and sat still, hoping to find that place of quiet again. God emerged from the stillness and gave me a new dream—an even better one.

Prayer

Lord, help me to remain still and ready to listen to You more. I ask that You give me the discipline to turn off my phone so I can hear You better when I pray. Thank You for always being there in the quiet of my room. Amen.

Day 10

There is Something Good in Store

> "For I know the plans I have for you," declares the Lord, "plans to prosper you and not to harm you, plans to give you hope and a future" (Jeremiah 29:11).

Everyone filed to the hall after church service for coffee and donuts. My daughter's friend wandered over and greeted me with a slight frown. I learned he prays daily, helps those in need, and tithes every Sunday. But he did not see how his efforts led to anything good in his life.

He struggled to find steady employment, which weighed him down with financial worries. We talked about God's desire to provide good things for him and how God's plan does not always line up with our expectations.

As my daughter's friend grabbed a donut and prepared to head home, I left him with one last thought: "Often, those who seem to have everything going for them were once the discouraged student, the unemployed, the financially broke, and the divorced."

Not everything will be good for a believer. Hardships will come. There cannot be the joy of glory without times of suffering. Our Savior faced this on the cross.

But God promises the pain and hardships will serve their purpose and contribute to an overall good in His plan for us. He wants His faithful to stay hopeful, never forgetting the goodness we seek is just beyond the rough circumstances for those who wait on the Lord.

Prayer

Lord, please help us see things differently, giving us hope even when there seems to be little joy in our lives at the moment. Amen.

Day 11

Water Station of Grace

> But we have this treasure in jars of clay to show that this all-surpassing power is from God and not from us (2 Corinthians 4:7).

We decided to venture out with the kids to a carnival before summer ended. The temperatures hovered around the mid-90s. We took a beating from the heat and humidity.

Hundreds of people waited in long lines for food and drinks. I gladly waited in line to refill everyone's water bottle. To run empty of water was the last thing I wanted to happen. I knew that dehydration sneaks up on humans if we do not stay alert. Our fragile bodies cannot go without water for long.

In 2 Corinthians, the Apostle Paul speaks of our bodies as jars of clay. His imagery reminds us we are weak and dependent on God. Our bodies are beautiful and functional—but oh, so fragile.

Even so, God provides a way around our frailty. He offers his thirst-quenching grace that strengthens our delicate bodies of clay and buffers us against pain and difficulties. And the more we understand our need for His drink, the more likely we will take precautions to stay spiritually hydrated.

The good news is we do not have to wait in a long line to replenish our clay jugs with spiritual water. The Holy Spirit will lead us to God's water station of grace when we make Christ first in our lives. Our participation in the mystery of Christ, through Sunday worship, daily prayer, and scripture reflection, allows His grace to flow unimpeded into our jars of clay. Our weaken bodies are strengthened and invigorated to take up the faith journey once again—pitfalls and all.

Prayer

Father, although I am fragile like a jar of clay, I am grateful for Your continuous wave of grace that proves our source of strength comes from You alone. Let me never take for granted Your gift of grace. Amen.

Day 12

Soaring the Skies

> *Through him all things were made; without him nothing was made that has been made (John 1:3).*

It is amazing how a huge Boeing 747 jumbo plane can soar among the clouds and defy the laws of gravity.

Think about it. The wings on the Boeing 747 extend 212 feet, and the engine weighs a massive 63,000 lbs. Not only that, but the entire Boeing 747 with passengers, cargo, and fuel might also weigh 875,000 lbs., which is the weight of 3,000 heavyweight wrestlers or over 400 tons.

Then, there's something scientists call the principle of lift. This principle, invented by God, occurs when the slower moving air below the wings becomes so strong that it can lift a giant 400-ton plane into the sky.

God is the master inventor. And when He made

each of us in His image, He gave us some of His special creative powers, allowing us to invent computers, phones, televisions, and even incredible flying things like the 400-ton Boeing 747.

When we paint, build, draw, write, sing, and many other creative activities, it shows God's creative powers working in us. He encourages you and me to use our creative abilities to make the world a better place for others.

Prayer

God, thank You for the inventions that make life better and more fun. I know with Your help, I can create something new one day. Amen.

Day 13

Trust the One Who Moves Mountains

> *Jesus looked at them and said, "With man this is impossible, but with God all things are possible"* (Matthew 19:26).

I read to my students about two incredible announcements from an angel of God. First, we went over the revelation by the angel to Zachariah. Then, the more incredible message we read about involved the Virgin Mary.

With each yearly reading of these verses during the Christmas season, I experienced an all-too-familiar reaction from the students—a willingness to listen along with a healthy amount of disbelief.

Even for the Virgin Mary, the announcement from God's angel, Gabriel, that she would bear the Son of

God left her wondering. And Zachariah's message on the unlikely birth of a child to his elderly wife prompted a similar reaction. But their answers to the angel revealed something even more telling.

Mary did not doubt the words of God, even though it seemed impossible. She trusted in the wisdom and power of her Lord. But Zachariah demanded proof. The announcement of the birth to his wife Elizabeth made no sense. Because of her advanced years, He doubted God's power to deliver on His word.

Elizabeth also had good reason to question God. But she never gave up hope and never hesitated to ask Him to intervene over and over. She endured many years of ridicule before the Lord blessed her by bringing forth the impossible, a son she named John the Baptist.

Both Mary and Elizabeth demonstrated the value of faith and perseverance in prayer. They believed in a superpower beyond what we consider normal. Without hope in the impossible, God's promises amount to only fairy tales.

But with faith and trust in the One who moves mountains, His gift of impossibilities, for all who continue to believe in them, can be witnessed even today if we make it a point to look for them.

Prayer

Father in heaven, give us the grace to believe in the impossible. Allow us to see the everyday miracles in our lives, and let us stand amazed at what You continue to do for us. Amen.

Children's children are a crown to the aged, and parents are the pride of their children (Proverbs 17:6).

Day 14

The Last Stop

> *My Father's house has many rooms; if that were not so, would I have told you that I am going there to prepare a place for you? (John 14:2).*

As I prepared to leave the kids at Grandma's house overnight, memories sprung up about my childhood camping trips and weekend sleepovers. My parents stuffed everything I needed in a duffel bag and prodded me out the front door. They reminded me to stay out of trouble, keep hydrated, and, of course, have fun.

The first few times away, I became homesick. I missed Mom and Dad and even my little sister, who did not know how to utter a word yet. All of us together made our house a home—a place filled with love and happiness.

As a husband and dad, I still suffer from homesickness now and then, especially when going on a business trip alone. But there was another kind of trip away that concerned me. It was the one-way journey we will all make one day, and the last stop ends at the front gate of the Kingdom of God.

Jesus hints that the separation time from the people we leave behind will last only awhile. Our Father in heaven promised to prepare a special place for us to gather once more, where loved ones will never be apart from us again on account of an unwanted business trip.

The place is the Father's house, and each room is made ready for us with love and care. No one becomes homesick there. Our heavenly Father longs for His faithful followers to reside with Him and experience perfect happiness forever. We are His daughters and sons. He wants us back safely with Him after our plight in this distant land ends.

Prayer

Father, thank You for promising to prepare a place for me in Your house. Since I often forget this world is not my home, I ask that You gently guide me to Your front doorstep when it is time to make my way back. Amen.

Day 15

The Best Choice

> *Look to the* LORD *and his strength; seek his face always. Remember the wonders he has done, his miracles, and the judgments he pronounced (1 Chronicles 16:11-12).*

Our kids were hungry. Again. We stopped at their favorite place to eat. They quickly pointed out a combo platter on the menu, which included everything they wanted. It seemed like a good pick. I presumed the combo platter would cost less than each item ordered separately.

Out of curiosity, I decided to add up the cost of each item to see how much I would save. But to my surprise, the combo platter was more expensive.

As Christians, we should likewise stop and calculate the spiritual cost before we make our choices. Decisions between good and evil can present challenges because of temptation. But when it comes to choosing from several good options, the decision often becomes even more difficult. In some way, the many good choices available distract us from seeing what is best.

God wants us to hold off on the combo platter to give us a chance to discover the best option. Instead, He prefers we select what He has in mind. And when we choose His will over our preferences, we have indeed chosen the best option.

Prayer

Heavenly Father, help me to choose to put Your Son and His will first, knowing it is the best choice I can make. Amen.

Day 16

Lost Touch

> *Then you will call on me and come and pray to me, and I will listen to you (Jeremiah 29:12).*

I overlooked something important.

Everything in my life was going well. The kids liked their school and friends. I enjoyed my career, and with a recent promotion, there came more income. Besides, the drive back from work barely took 10 minutes, which gave me more time to spend with the family.

After dinner, I stretched out in my favorite lounge chair and made plans for the weekend. I scribbled down a list of things to do and discovered not only something missing from my list—but from my everyday life.

With a life filled with the kids' school activities, soccer games, and nine holes of golf on the weekends, I gave little attention to prayer. I disregarded God's importance and failed to recognize His care and blessings in our lives.

Without prayer, we lose touch with God and eventually fail to notice Him anymore in our lives.

Prayer is central to our faith as Christians. It strengthens our relationship with Him. He waits to hear from us each day. Prayer helps us to understand His will for us, and it opens our hearts to witness His actions working in our lives. Our faith deepens as we tune in to God.

God wants us to make prayer a treasured activity. It is the perfect remedy against indifference towards the One who provides all good things.

Prayer

Lord, never let us lose touch with You. Remind us that no matter what circumstances we find ourselves in, You are only a prayer away—eager to listen and help. Amen.

Day 17

Rejoice!

> *Rejoice in the Lord always. I will say it again: Rejoice! Let your gentleness be evident to all. The Lord is near* (Philippians 4:4-5).

I drove up the last stretch of winding road to the cabin. The last few months, filled with unwanted surprises and worries, wore me down. I needed a getaway to recoup and regain my balance. "Now that we're here, do you feel relaxed?" asked my wife.

The change in scenery did not help. The worries returned. My ability to cope with the circumstances stood out of reach, with thoughts torn in so many directions. In Philippians, Apostle Paul speaks of rejoicing in the Lord always. He does not suggest we delight in the tragic events in our lives, but rejoice in Jesus Christ, our Redeemer, while amid the storm.

We can rejoice when life turns against us. Because, in our troubles, Christ is close, and in our friendship with Him, there is hope. The Lord does not want the sorrows to break our hearts. Times of struggles are the times to hold on tighter. Stay in the race. He cheers us on to finish what we started. It is a race where we will be victorious in the end.

Jesus died for us, and He rose on the third day. Upon this truth of the resurrection, our joy must originate. Rejoice in Him always.

Prayer

Lord, we thank You for Your friendship. Help me to rest and rejoice in You and the gift of salvation during times of trouble and hardship. Amen.

Day 18

Walk a Little Slower

> *This is the account of Noah and his family. Noah was a righteous man, blameless among the people of his time, and he walked faithfully with God (Genesis 6:9).*

She gave me a model to follow.

As we touched down, the Boeing 747 bobbed down the runway amid the flickering lights. The plane joggled to a stop. Passengers grabbed coats and bags from the overhead compartments and crammed the aisle to deplane. I continued to rummage under the front seat for a missing pink sneaker.

My daughter and I finally exited the plane and headed for the confines of the terminal. "It's better to walk a little slower, Daddy," she shouted. "I don't want to fall." My daughter often reminded me I was leading her, and my steps were too fast.

She's all grown-up now and married. But I remember how she followed me everywhere, believing I was able to guide her safely through the circumstances. She followed when I escorted her to school on the first day of kindergarten; she followed when I stepped into the doctor's office for her to receive shots, and she followed when I led her to the edge of the pool for our first dip together.

But unlike my daughter, I like to lead most of the time and control my destiny. I even find myself interrupting God, believing He would follow me. Then I shamelessly begged for help when things didn't go as planned.

In truth, we can't entirely control our destiny. Our knowledge and understanding are limited—and we have a sinful nature, too.

The rightful one to lead is our Maker. The same one who led Noah. The one who holds the knowledge of the past, present, and future events in concert. He who leads us safely through our storms, our fears, our losses.

If we are to become followers, the requirement is trust in Him. We humbly follow, knowing He will guide us in the right direction. And to help, God gives us His footsteps to follow and asks that we not yield to the temptation to rush ahead—alone.

My daughter's words, way back when, are still a reminder to walk slower because we may fall.

Let Christ set the pace for you each day.

Prayer

Jesus, help me to see this world in the way You see things. I am so eager to set my own pace in this hectic world that I often forget to slow down and follow You. Amen.

Day 19

Another Blunder

> *If you, Lord, kept a record of sins, Lord, who could stand? But with you there is forgiveness, so that we can, with reverence, serve you (Psalm 130:3-4).*

The supervisor kept a record.

Early in my career as a new hire, my supervisor required all the trainees to follow a strict set of standards. During the review of our work, he jagged his finger at our errors and highlighted them with his red marking pen. Even with nothing said, I still heard a snarl amid the strokes of his red pen.

It seemed he documented our mistakes in his logbook for posterity. The blunder log—as we employees called it—added to the pressure we already carried. The prevention of any slip-ups was more critical to our supervisor than our growth and success. We focused on staying clear of mistakes at the expense of our personal development.

Unlike the supervisor, God does not tally our blunders in a logbook or entangle us in shame. Instead, He encourages us, offers us a new beginning, and promises to remember our sins no more. He takes an interest in the vocations He calls us to fulfill.

God is our model for guiding our children, friends, and colleagues with forgiveness and compassion—a model we ought not to overlook. He wants us to display a similar level of care in our lives, where we reassure each other and pick up those who have fallen.

We can thank God for not keeping a logbook of our mistakes and for the safe place in Him that allows us to grow from our mistakes without fear. His loving support gives us the self-confidence to push on, especially when we find it difficult to do so on our own.

Bless those around you by not keeping a log of their blunders.

Prayer

Father, You know our sins and blunders—every single one of them. I thank You for putting them aside and giving us another opportunity to do better. I am grateful for Your grace and loving encouragement. Amen.

Day 20

Seeds of Faith

> *Therefore go and make disciples of all nations, baptizing them in the name of the Father and of the Son and of the Holy Spirit (Matthew 28:19).*

I kept silent. Again.

I arrived at the office at 6:30 a.m. and scurried over to the breakroom for coffee to jump-start my day. As I dumped creamer into my coffee, I overheard two colleagues discussing their daughter's clothing choices. "My parents would have never allowed me to dress the way they do these days," said one of them. "It's too showy for my taste." But they did not think it caused any real harm.

Even though I believe we needed to teach our children about modesty, I did not say a word. I dreaded the idea of offending them and getting labeled as a narrow-minded Christian around the office.

Jesus told His disciples not to be afraid and stay committed to their mission. His words to them are words to us, too. He did not command us to tolerate any view someone may have. Instead, Christ wants us to live out His teachings faithfully and make disciples of all nations—even if it means ruffling some feathers along the way.

God reminds us to be faithful followers and allow our Christian light to shine. We are His messengers. And this involves telling others about Jesus Christ and His life-changing message—a message our colleagues and friends may find unpleasant.

When we courageously share the Christian message, we plant seeds of faith, and God brings forth the harvest.

Become a mirror of Christ. Be a courageous seeder of your faith.

Prayer

Jesus, teach me to be a more courageous disciple. When it is time to speak up with kindness about my faith, let me not hesitant because of fear. Amen.

Day 21

Imaginary Characters

> *"Be careful," Jesus warned them. "Watch out for the yeast of the Pharisees and that of Herod."* (Mark 8:15).

When our adult children went off on their own to live, they left behind boxes of childhood possessions. One box filled with superhero getups, Halloween masks, and princess dresses caught my attention. The kids spent hours in their costumes, pretending to be their favorite imaginary characters.

Children who play-act in their fantasy worlds are delightful. But to pretend, in an attempt to grab power and esteem, is not an honorable act. God does not want us trapped in our make-believe characters at the expense of our true Christian identities.

Our Lord cautions that the Pharisees, whom He refers to as hypocrites, pretend to be someone they are not. The religious leaders cared about external appearances and what people thought of them but failed to pay attention to something more important: the state of their souls.

God values the hidden things deep in our hearts—such as integrity, virtue, and humility. Jesus warns against the use of an imaginary self as a way to misrepresent who we are. He wants you and me to stop acting out of selfish ambition.

Let us begin to resist the enticement of power and fame that often draws us far away from the love of the Father. We cannot fulfill His will when we operate as posers in pursuit of self-love and power. Honor Him with a renewed commitment to stay unpretentious in our dealings with others—and our Father in heaven will honor us.

Prayer

Lord, guard me against the temptation to manipulate others to get what I want fast. And provide me the grace to prevent selfishness from consuming my life such that I fail to reach out in love to You or those in need of help. Amen.

Day 22

Directions

> *I will instruct you and teach you in the way you should go; I will counsel you with my loving eye on you (Psalm 32:8).*

Do not forget your road map.

My eldest son dropped by for dinner to discuss his upcoming cross-country drive to Charlotte, North Carolina. His plans included the people he wanted to visit and the places he hoped to see. The trip would cover over 2,500 miles. I asked him to consider a road map to help plot a course. He shot me a double take. "Dad, do people still have maps?" he said. "I thought everyone used GPS on their phones."

I went on to boast about how I had used a map to drive 47 hours from San Diego to New York City way back when. When I needed assistance, I stopped at gas stations for directions, and strangers, pumping gas, offered to help: "I'm going in that direction. Just follow me."

We talked about how GPS works great for "turn left in 3.8 miles" when faced with a choice to either turn at the signal or down a side street. But I recognized any attempt to chart a trip on our phones would challenge even the most skilled navigator. The phone screen limits the full view of the route—which makes it difficult to keep sight of our destination.

Before my son departed, I reminded him to take the road map I gave him—and, of course, to stay hydrated. With the dog settled in the back seat and the road map positioned next to the water bottle, I was now ready to wish him a great journey. We waved goodbye.

Our Christian voyage requires that we chart a course and exercise a bird's-eye view. When we place too much trust on a narrow vision of things, like the view we see on our phones, our perspective gets twisted. We forget our destination does not end in this world, and the joy we seek remains beyond the horizon.

Jesus wants us to stop at the nearest gas station and ask Him for directions when we find ourselves confused at a crossroads. He is the gentlemen pumping gas who says, "Follow me." He certainly knows the way and wants to get us back on track.

Jesus is our way through this fallen world and is the best road map to get us from here to there. But detours abound when we attempt to navigate an unknown course on our own. He understands our spiritual journey can be made simpler if we ask for directions and allow Him to lead the way.

Prayer

O God, help us to put aside our efforts at navigating through this fallen world alone. Let me be humble enough to stop and ask for directions from You. Amen.

Day 23

Time to Let Go

> But the worries of this life, the deceitfulness of wealth and the desires for other things come in and choke the word, making it unfruitful (Mark 4:19).

My wife and I needed a better approach.

With the kids out of the house, we took the risk and moved to a smaller place. The move became a real challenge. *How are we going to make everything fit in our new tiny home?* I wondered. *What should we keep, and what should we toss or donate?*

I struggled with these questions as I sifted through our things. I marked the item "keep" when I no longer needed it. And other items I marked "toss," when, in fact, I needed them. I did not have a clue.

With prayer and some research, I settled on a strategy. I tossed out everything I would never use again. I donated items others could use and kept items needed at the new place—including sentimental items we would enjoy for years to come.

As Christians, we, too, need a spiritual strategy to toss out the things that push us away from God and keep only the things that pull us toward Him. I put together an inventory of what I valued and discovered the possessions, people, and activities that affected my life in Christ.

An over-packed schedule, coupled with a need for the extras of this secular world, weakened the union I had with Christ. God wants us to avoid the earthly clutter that blocks our way to His Son. He wants us to resist being charmed by the glitter of city lights and the potpourri of neon signs—some of the things the world uses to distract us. In its place, He wants us to seek only Jesus' dazzling light that shines in the deep niches of a believer's heart.

God celebrates every sacrifice we make to release the things in our lives for His sake. Take a spiritual inventory and eliminate anything that gets in the way of a deeper relationship with Christ.

Prayer

Lord Jesus, please come into our hearts and homes and remove anything that may become a stumbling block to You. Amen.

Day 24

Hold on to Hope

> *And the God of all grace, who called you to his eternal glory in Christ, after you have suffered a little while, will himself restore you and make you strong, firm and steadfast (1 Peter 5:10).*

I had to stay off my feet for a few days.

My knee was pounding with pain as I limped from room to room. As I sat stranded in front of the TV and bore the discomfort, a homebound friend from church came to mind. He always offered a cheerful smile when I dropped in for a visit. Even on days filled with severe pain, he extended his hand to greet me— but he uttered not a word. I understood what his silence meant and prayed for his pain to go away.

His witness to the power of God's grace, which sustained him through his many trials, inspired me and strengthened my faith. I was there to cheer him up, but often it looked as if I got cheered up instead.

Our friends and family members, who inspire us in the face of illness, should remind us to hold tight to Christ during the storm. God wants us to find hope in Him, who cares about every difficulty. He was there when we grieved and mourned and cried out in pain. Jesus knows our hardships. He certainly felt them before.

The Lord does not want our trust in Him undermined, allowing despair to strip us of hope. There is hope in Jesus. But hopelessness is just around the corner for anyone wanting to go it alone.

Encouraged by those who maintain hope in times of suffering, we must seek to sustain hope while in a struggle by always going to the One who heals and comforts.

Prayer

Lord, at times, it seems impossible to feel hopeful during our trials. Help us trust in and through You that we regain the hope we very much need. Amen.

Day 25

Opinions

> *My sheep listen to my voice; I know them, and they follow me. I give them eternal life, and they shall never perish; no one will snatch them out of my hand (John 10:27-28).*

We were on high alert!

As my wife and I braced for a visit from our new in-laws, we noticed things around the house that did not bother us before. The dinner plates seemed old and dull, the windows did not shine brightly enough, and the hardwood floors squeaked at too many places.

We assumed the small imperfections around the house would be detected by our guests of honor. The saying, "Good appearance makes for a good impression," bellowed in my head. I was worn out, especially from all the closet cramming and furniture shuffling going on.

Even our cherished rose garden we had tilled and pruned the week before became a source of worry. As I sat and gazed at a blossom of red and white roses—wondering how I was going to get everything done—it hit me how my life hinges on the opinions of others.

The need to hear the voice of approval from friends and colleagues, and even family members, consumed a lot of my thoughts, which did not leave much room to hear from Him. I allowed the opinions of ordinary people to disturb my whole day.

God does not want us held captive by the opinions and criticisms of those around us that we forget who we are as His sons and daughters. He wants us to live as the persons He brought us into the world to be, where we seek His approval and thoughts and words of encouragement.

God's word should matter most. The views of others may seem like a good barometer for measuring our successes and failures. But in the end, only God's word is trustworthy. Only in Him are we freed from the hold others may have on us.

Free yourself from the opinions of others by seeking only the voice of your Shepherd.

Prayer

Lord, help us from living our lives based solely on the opinions of those around us. Let us trust You alone, knowing only You can rightfully guide us in our choices. Amen.

Day 26

Change of Plans

> *Give thanks in all circumstances; for this is God's will for you in Christ Jesus (1 Thessalonians 5:18).*

Our daughter alerted us a few weeks in advance whenever she needed us to watch her pups. But since we did not hear from her, my wife and I booked a room for the long 4th of July weekend.

On the night before our out-of-town trip, we received a phone call. "Dad, I need a favor," said my daughter. "Can you watch the pups over the weekend?" She described the emergency at her house. We canceled our long weekend plans.

A blessing in disguise, as the old saying goes, when we received the phone call from her that evening. As it turned out, the news reported the next morning that a brush fire erupted at the resort we planned to visit. Deaths reported. Authorities ordered visitors to turn back. Those who drove up a day earlier became stranded because of the many road closures.

We enjoyed our time with the pups over the 4th of July weekend, and we are grateful that God stepped in and juggled our weekend plans.

Trust the Lord's providence. The unforeseen changes to our plans often reveal the work of the Lord. He works this way. With trust and faith, we will come to praise Him for putting up those barriers. He sees what we cannot see—the threatening tinder fires ahead. God closes roads for justified reasons and will never reopen them a moment too soon.

Prayer

Lord, help me to trust in Your providence when unforeseen circumstances force me to change plans. And give me the strength to resist the temptation to push headlong when You signal roads closed ahead. Amen.

Day 27

Please Wait

> *Yet the Lord longs to be gracious to you; therefore he will rise up to show you compassion. For the Lord is a God of justice. Blessed are all who wait for him! (Isaiah 30:18).*

The busier the day got, the more I waited.

I waited in traffic, I waited in the checkout line, and I waited in line for gas. I even waited at a restaurant with a "No Waiting" sign. I fell behind schedule and resented others for making me wait.

If I had remembered He was in control, I would have handled the delays better. God offers His peace to those who wait. His timing is perfect and certainly an improvement over the schedule I scribbled down that day.

I forgot about the all-important virtue of patience as I stood stranded in line. God wants faithful and patient followers. Staying on schedule is a good thing, but we need to trust Him when delays intrude on our time. He often has a good reason for them.

God will achieve His purpose, whether we like it or not. Instead of trying to control others and circumstances when we know it is not possible, we should trust His change in plans—no matter what happens and no matter how long we must wait.

When we remember God's flawless timing, the delays become bearable and serve as signs to readjust our lives to His plan. With the help of God's grace, we can find patience again—even amid a world filled with fast food and express lanes.

With trust in God, we permit ourselves to wait for Him and prepare for a better way, which are the moments of delay before God asks us to make a change.

Wait patiently today so we can experience the peace of God.

Prayer

O God, help us to embrace the virtue of patience. And give us faith to skip items on our "To Do" list in favor of the changes You usher into our day. Amen.

Day 28

Heritage Remembered

> *This is what the LORD says: "When seventy years are completed for Babylon, I will come to you and fulfill my good promise to bring you back to this place. (Jeremiah 29:10).*

They needed a refresher.

My wife and I arrived at the party hall to celebrate a family member's golden wedding anniversary. Gold helium balloons, gold-glittered flowers in gold vases, and even gold-lined tablecloths decked the banquet room.

Our adult children attended, too. Considering their meager five years of marriage experience among them, it oddly made sense that our children would be curious about how fifty years of marriage looked.

A few septuagenarians attending the celebration

stopped by our table for a chat. It was a long time since we last saw them. We talked about the old days. They rattled off the names of family members, past and present. The elders believed it was a must to know and share one's heritage.

Not recognizing most of the names, our children wanted to hear more about their ancestors. They lost track of their family connections and, in some sense, forgot who they were. We reminisced about the lives of some of the relatives at the party. My wife and I also talked about their great-grandparents, whom they never met.

This look-back reminded me of the Israelites' return from Babylon after seventy years of captivity. When they returned to their homeland, the Israelites needed, as our children did, a refresher on who they were. Reflecting on their heritage, the Israelites rediscovered their identity as God's chosen people.

As children of God, reflection upon our Christian heritage often—and with gratitude—is needed. We should never lose track of who we are and what it means to belong to the family of God. Being a member of His household affords us many gifts and the promise of eternal life with Jesus Christ. God will certainly keep His promise to us as He kept His word to the Israelites.

Invite someone to be part of Jesus Christ's family today.

Prayer

Lord, thank You for making us Your sons and daughters. May the lost in this world respond to Your invitation to be part of Your family. Through Jesus, Amen.

Day 29

Holiday Challenge

> *Come to me, all you who are weary and burdened, and I will give you rest. Take my yoke upon you and learn from me, for I am gentle and humble in heart, and you will find rest for your souls (Matthew 11:28-29).*

After our kids moved out of the house, the stress of Christmas shopping tapered off. The children also decided to end a longstanding tradition of giving us a Christmas list to labor over, which certainly helped ease our holiday worries.

Even with a lighter Christmas shopping load, I still grumbled as I struggled to pick out gift cards for family members and friends. As I drove home, I stopped at a crosswalk and waited for a frail gentleman to hobble across the street. He wore ripped clothes. His face emptied of life.

It struck me that my holiday challenges were insignificant compared to many others.

For those going through hard times, the Christmas season represents an extra burden to an already overburdened life. The holidays are often a blunt reminder of a lost job, a medical condition, or a shattered relationship—a life seemingly without hope.

But in Christ, there is hope. Our Lord has endless compassion for those who carry a heavy heart. He invites us to come to Him, like a child in need of reassurance that things will be all right.

God is our reassuring parent who helps restores hope. He wants us to tether our lives to His yoke to lessen the weight we try to carry alone. He understands our circumstances and is eager to help us when life becomes extra hard.

God does not want us to lug around our heavy burdens by ourselves. Accept His invitation to come to Him, trusting He will provide hope during the trying times and rest when the soul becomes weary.

Prayer

Father, forgive us for depending on ourselves more than on You at times. I thank You for coming into my life and helping me carry my load. Give us humility to accept Your offer of hope and rest when we need it the most. Amen.

Day 30

The First Christmas Over 2000 Years Ago

> *Today in the town of David a Savior has been born to you; he is the Messiah, the Lord. This will be a sign to you: You will find a baby wrapped in cloths and lying in a manger (Luke 2:11-12).*

We finally finished decorating the Christmas tree. The six-foot Douglas fir twinkled with red, green, and blue lights, and the lights glistened off the baubles and tinsel. Tired and hungry from the decorating, we sat down for a quick bite. "Daddy, why do we put up Christmas decorations?" asked my seven-year-old son.

I scanned the house for something amongst the decorations to help me answer his question. Along with the Christmas tree, we adorned the house with wreaths, presents, lights, and Christmas stockings.

To my surprise, not a single decoration conveyed the Christmas message I hoped to find.

With all the hustle and bustle, I neglected to include Jesus in our Christmas celebration. My focus was on decorating the house, shopping for presents, and preparing for parties.

God does not want us so consumed by holiday activities that we fail to remember the precious gift we received at Christmas. On this day, over 2000 years ago, Mary gave birth to Jesus, wrapped Him in swaddling clothes, and placed our Savior in a manger. The birth of Jesus ushered in a new way of life in Christ and a blessed eternal life to come.

God would like us to fill our homes and Christmas activities with things that remind us of the importance of Christmas—things that direct our hearts to our Savior's birth in the humble town of Bethlehem.

Let us focus on the greatness of the birth of Jesus—and not only at Christmas.

Prayer

Lord, help me to treasure Your miracle on Christmas Day. And remind me to keep my gaze on You, even when the Christmas season becomes too busy. I thank You for coming into our world as a human to save us. Amen.

And they said, "Believe in the Lord Jesus, and you will be saved, you and your household." And they spoke the word of the Lord to him and to all who were in his house. And he took them the same hour of the night and washed their wounds, and he was baptized at once, he and all his family. Then he brought them up into his house and set food before them. And he rejoiced along with his entire household that he had believed in God (Acts 16:31-34 ESV).

www.ingramcontent.com/pod-product-compliance
Lightning Source LLC
Chambersburg PA
CBHW071025080526
44587CB00015B/2509